# CHI
# ONLINE

## social media

**LAURA TRENEER**

BRF

**The Bible Reading Fellowship**
15 The Chambers, Vineyard
Abingdon OX14 3FE
brf.org.uk

The Bible Reading Fellowship (BRF) is a Registered Charity (233280)

ISBN 978 0 85746 557 3
First published 2017
10 9 8 7 6 5 4 3 2 1 0
All rights reserved

## Acknowledgements

Scripture quotations taken from The Holy Bible, New International
Version (Anglicised edition) copyright © 1979, 1984, 2011 by
Biblica. Used by permission of Hodder & Stoughton Publishers,
a Hachette UK company. All rights reserved. 'NIV' is a registered
trademark of Biblica. UK trademark number 1448790.

A catalogue record for this book is available from the British Library

Printed and bound by CPI Group (UK) Ltd, Croydon CR0 4YY

# Contents

Introduction                          4

1. Why it matters                     7

2. What to consider first            38

3. Essential next steps              55

4. Toolkit                           82

Notes                                91

'Balanced, supportive, encouraging,
practical… A total thumbs up!'

Dr Bex Lewis, author of *Raising Children in a Digital Age*

'An essential resource for all
church leaders.'

Jo Swinney, editor of *Preach* magazine

# Introduction

No resource on church communication and outreach would be complete without proper attention to social media. It can no longer be considered niche, or only for the young (if it ever was). One book on ministry in the digital age describes us as being in a 'post-website world'.[1] Social media is part of the fabric of how we speak, listen to, understand and relate to our friends and neighbours. It is mainstream.

*'I feel like my church should be doing more on social media.'*

*'I use social media—my church should do it better.'*

*'Perhaps I should do something about it.'*

The word 'should' comes up frequently when we talk to UK churches about social media. Whether you're slightly compulsive on Facebook, a recent convert to Instagram, or sceptical about all social media, there will be others in your church who feel differently. This isn't a book that tells you it's a sin if your church isn't on Facebook. There is no strong agenda about the tools your church should use. You just need the knowledge to move confidently in a way that fits your community and your communications as a whole. Social media, after all, is only a tool. It's not good or bad. Like any tool, it's what you do with it that counts.

This series of books starts from the understanding that it is God's nature to communicate. He is the first and the best communicator. Being made in his image means we're equipped to take part. Digital tools are a gift for this—and so are all the traditional church communication methods, but they're more effective when used together. Churches can run all sorts of events and groups, but it's a waste of time if no one hears about them. This is where digital communication comes into its own.

Churches have an immense opportunity! Not only do they get to be places of sacramental worship, teaching, communion, fellowship and all those other words that are understood by most UK Christians, but not necessarily by their neighbours. They also get to be lights in their community and centres of communication about what it is to be a follower of Christ.

Churches get to ask the big questions in the public sphere. Through every means of communication we have available to us—buildings, services, ministries, websites, printed invitations, social media, videos, magazines, news sheets, noticeboards, the smiles on our faces, the words out of our mouths—churches can fundamentally change perceptions of Jesus Christ and of those who believe he still has the power to change lives.

This series is for those who feel responsibility for church communications and for those who think it makes a difference. There is plenty that the world of corporate and charity marketing can teach the church. Free resources are more readily available than ever before.

Hopefully the tools in these books will help you form a simple strategy and plan that starts squarely in the reality of your situation. It's written so that the intimidated can relax, the curious can explore and the goal-oriented can focus.

# 1

# Why it matters

In 2016 the social media manager for the Salvation Army, David Giles, asked hundreds of people of faith (not just Christians) whether their faith leaders actively encouraged them to use social media to discuss spiritual matters. Almost half said yes. If you're a church leader, are you one of those who encourages this use? Over *three-quarters* of Christian survey respondents felt that social media is an appropriate platform from which to talk about their faith. They rarely or never receive any critical reaction from their readers for doing so.[2]

What we see from this is that, whatever the level of your church's engagement with social media, it is probably already being used intentionally, prayerfully and even evangelistically by those in your congregation.

## Five opportunities

Here are five simple reasons churches can get excited about social media and know, without doubt, that it relates to them, whether used by the church or not:

# 1. It can reach places other methods can't reach

There is the opportunity to share, to listen, to create conversation, to find common ground. For people starting a church from scratch, local social media activity can be a very quick way to reach thousands. For events it provides cheap, effective publicity. People telling their stories of faith, particularly in creative ways or using video or images, will reach an audience possibly greater than any they'd find in church on a Sunday morning.[3]

Social media enables the message of Jesus to go into parts of the world where missionaries are not welcome. It can be the feet and voice of the church worldwide without leaving the kitchen table.

## 2. It connects us to our neighbours

A group at the University of Durham, CODEC, focuses its research on theological engagement with new media. In a paper written in June 2013, lead researcher Pete Phillips wrote this:

*Because of the way that digital communication transcends the geographical and the physical, transcends even the limitations of time and presence,* *it can also be used to **augment what the church is already doing**—to connect us all as part of a whole community.*[4]

Since this paper was written, digital communication, and social media in particular, has become ever more integral to how our communities function and develop. Academic research into 'digital religion' has shown that church online activity can be most effective when it supplements 'offline' activity rather than seeking to replace it. It reaches those who may not connect to traditional church.[5]

## 3. It can increase fellowship

For all the potential irritation of endless shared photos of new babies, sun-kissed beaches or barbecue food, social media can help us reveal our wider lives to those who would otherwise see us only in one context. It can forge unexpected connections and increase transparency in relationships.

In churches, it gives equal presence to those shut in to their homes by illness, age or disability. It means that missionaries in other places can stay visibly connected.

Brandon Cox, editor of www.pastors.com, writes this:

*How do we give a cup of cold water in Jesus' name online? In other words, how do we truly serve people in hands-on ways when we aren't sharing the same physical space? The answer has to do with the encouragement vacuum that exists in our culture. Because the internet has turned us all into publishers, harsh opinions and cynical thoughts dominate social networks. But God's people, changed by the radical grace of Jesus, get to enter that void with genuine love and encouragement.*[6]

In other words, Christians have an opportunity in social media for encouragement beyond limitations of proximity. Dr Bex Lewis, who trains church leaders in effective use of social media, says, 'When I'm training churches in social media I like to challenge people on what the fruits of the Spirit listed in Galatians look like online. How can we integrate these kinds of discussions into sermons?'

## 4. It can increase discovery, learning and spiritual growth

The enormous popularity of TED talks (short talks of 18 minutes or less on Technology, Entertainment and Design, online at conferences)[7] has shown that there is a hunger for learning, for public speaking, for the kind of mini lectures or short talks on meaningful topics that Christians can take for granted from a steady diet of preaching. Our generation has access to the largest ever free resource of talks, courses, Bibles, commentaries, videos and discipleship resources online. We're spoilt. Social media helps us discover ('curate') what we need, seek recommendations and comment.

Elizabeth Drescher writes about what she calls the 'Digital Reformation'. She says, 'There's an incredible opportunity to participate in making more public and visible what for the last 500 years has been a largely invisible, privatised practice of faith.'[8] The Church of England has expressed this with live services every week over Twitter, Periscope and other streams.

Have you ever read something fresh and longed to tell someone? Have you ever had a spiritual breakthrough or a eureka moment of understanding, not in church, but as a result of your own exploration? Have you ever seen something incredible and caught it on your phone's camera? Have you ever read something quickly on Facebook or Twitter and been surprised at the way it sticks in your head, reverberates around your soul, awakens a sense of recognition?

The amazing thing is that when this happens (and if it hasn't happened to you, hold out—it can), you can tell someone. Even if you're standing on your own with a dodgy 3G connection in the middle of the countryside, you can celebrate the discovery. We can shout about the gems. Pioneer vicar Robin Ham talks about this in *Unfiltered Grace*, a book about Instagram, as 'a desire to declare, to praise, possibly even because we've lost sight of a God to praise and thank'.[9] Social media is another place where we can talk about the reality of faith in a way that is authentic and integrated into the rest of our lives.

In 2014, research in the Midlands on 'what helps disciples grow' found that 10% were helped by online discussions, including on social media, and 36% were helped by listening to Christian teaching, including online (although online listening wasn't distinguished from radio or video).[10]

The same study found that fewer than half claimed to be helped by church services. We know that there are many thousands seeking to grow in their faith outside church. Social media provides an introduction and access to individual tools for learning.

Ultimately everything around us can increase discovery, learning and spiritual growth. Perhaps it's just that our expectations of social media are too low.

## 5. It's everywhere, it's changing the way the next generation relate, and it's here to stay

A snapshot of the world's population in 2016 showed:

- 51% use a mobile phone
- 46% use the internet—up 10% in a year
- 31% use social media—up 10% in a year
- 27% use social media on their phone—up 17%

Facebook reaches 1.5 billion people and can control what appears on anyone's 'wall' to the extent that many organisations, including charities and churches, are finding they need to pay to guarantee they're seen.

Instagram's photo and video sharing app is increasing in popularity faster than Facebook, with almost half its users aged under 25.

WhatsApp, used for private group chats on smartphones, grew by 50% in 2016 alone.

As for the UK, there are more mobile phones than people. Over half of the population uses their phone for social media. Government statistics for 2015 showed that social networking was used by 61% of adults, and of those, 79% used it daily. Interestingly, this includes 44% of those aged 55–64.[11] It's not just the young, although they're far more likely to use their phone than a computer. It's not niche, or new, or developing. It's ingrained, permanent, the 'electricity of modern society and commerce, connecting us to the people and things we care about most'.[12]

The shift towards personal private chat tools—Facebook Messenger, WhatsApp, Snapchat—has shown that social media is increasingly viewed as an individual relationship tool, not just a public persona. People still trust personal recommendations—conversations about organisations, including churches—more than anything else.

As people spend more time online, the assumption is that any physical organisation will have a digital mirror. It's easier to search digitally, so if you don't have a digital mirror, do you in fact exist at all? As the Diocese of York social media guidelines put it: 'Not having a website or a Facebook page is like not having a church building in a town: people cannot come to us if we're not there.'[13]

This doesn't need to be a threat. History is full of examples of situations where the church has exploited new tools and technology to God's glory. As one tweet put it:

*Clay tablet… scroll… blackboard… print… pencil… pictures… comic… video… web. Same Word… changing medium #digichild*[14]

Justin Wise, in his book *The Social Church*, compares social media to Luther's use of the printing press to remove the 'gatekeepers' and spread God's word.[15] To keep our head in the sand is to choose to be culturally ignorant.

If you think your faith is relevant to your culture… if you think the church has a voice worth hearing… if you think a community of people is worth reaching… then it won't be enough to read this book. You will see the need for your church to re-evaluate its communication almost constantly in the context of a shifting digital landscape.

This doesn't mean jumping on every bandwagon or abandoning the timeless quality of worship in your setting. It means keeping your ear to the ground and making conscious choices about what you choose to adopt or only to observe.

The excellent 2015 book *Virtually Human* considers how Christians can be 'reflective practitioners':

*Technology is like a frame through which we see the world, which then becomes the world we live… If we are unthinking about its real impact on us and think of it as 'just a tool', [are] we blind to its true power?*[16]

Engaging with the world thoughtfully can help us engage more thoughtfully with our identity in Christ.

In 2016, one survey found that half of church leaders encouraged social media use. In a report written four years earlier, this proportion was far lower,[17] so clearly it's a growing vision, and one that surely requires more strategic encouragement and practical resources.

So, these are five reasons why social media matters:

1. It can reach places other methods can't reach.
2. It connects us to our neighbours.
3. It can increase fellowship.
4. It can increase discovery, learning and spiritual growth.
5. It's everywhere, it's changing the way the next generation relate, and it's here to stay.

If nothing else, this list shows that social media is already part of your church, whether you have an 'official presence' or not. Your members use it. Their friends use it. Anyone under 25 won't know how not to use it. The question is how to harness it to serve your common purpose, not in a tokenistic way, but with purpose and even pleasure.

## Nine reasons people don't bother

You'll notice, if you read the other books in this series, that some of the following are the same as the reasons people don't bother with websites and other forms of digital communication. Not a coincidence! There is some overlap. Even if these are never reasons you'd use, you may hear them from others.

## 1. Too complicated?

It can be; it doesn't need to be.

The mechanics of actually communicating on social media as a church can be extremely simple if your motivation is focused and you have the right team in place. This book aims to give you a simple strategy for this.

The complication is sometimes inside our own minds. How can I think differently? How can I incorporate into my mindset such a radically different mode of communication? I'm not in 'Generation Y'! If the level of interaction, sharing and boundary-blurring of social media feels, well, discombobulating, don't fret. You don't necessarily need to be the person doing this on behalf of your church. Your very being is not under threat. And as you read, you may find that it's actually far less complicated than you fear.

Neil Pugmire, in *100 Ways to Get Your Church Noticed*,[18] uses three helpful words to summarise churches and social media: dialogue, immediacy and networks. Churches reaching out to their communities are already developing networks, engaging in dialogue, and relating with immediacy and present-mindedness. Social media can just make this easier.

## 2. Too exposing?

This is a related fear—that social media somehow exposes our weaknesses in a way that other communication tools don't. Church leaders may feel that by being networked online they will be called on to respond to everything going on in the lives of their congregation. They will be exposed to people's lives outside their Sunday personas, filters off, and this may create expectations that are perhaps too high to fulfil.

This is one of the reasons why many church leaders eschew Facebook in particular. It requires discernment to know how to pastorally approach situations that you and hundreds of others have glimpsed in a passing newsfeed, let alone the posts hidden behind endless advertising. If a church leader sees a photo revealing someone's other side, or an angry discussion of political views, for example, at what point do they respond? Conversely, is this the place for them to show their own personal photos or convictions that they wouldn't include in a sermon?

Everyone—including church leaders—needs to make their own call about where they choose to be present. If members of a church are on social media, it's something that can be talked about on a Sunday, because it's part of people's daily lives, whether or not the preacher can relate to it. Should we only be on social media if we feel comfortable with it? Should we only be present where we're comfortable?

Followers of Jesus have always gone into places that others might consider slightly scary. Perhaps, for some in your church, social media can seem overwhelming, or a place where 'trolls' seek to abuse

Christians. As mentioned earlier, though, David Giles found that 70% of people rarely or never received a negative reaction, let alone abuse, for speaking about their faith on social media. You can always hide or ignore comments you don't like, or block people. Yes—social media can be exposing. But perhaps that's actually a good thing.

There is a related concern here, however—which is that it's too risky in terms of safeguarding.

Safeguarding is one area where churches online can be exposed by not seeking advice, or by failing to employ the common sense and guidelines they'd use in 'offline' safeguarding. For example, in a church setting, a responsible adult would never take unknown children into a private area on their own. Similar principles apply online. There is a list of excellent guidelines in Chapter 4 (Toolkit) for social media among vulnerable adults and children, which address this concern.

## 3. We're too old to learn?

The generational divide within churches is never more obvious than in the area of digital communication, but it is easy to make wrong assumptions based on age.

The age group growing fastest in their use of the internet is those aged 65–74. Men are more active than women. Photos of new grandchildren: what a great incentive to get online! It's those slightly older, over 75, who are far less likely to be online (among whom half of men and two thirds of women have never used the internet.)[19] If you consider that a third of the Church of England is aged over 70, it goes some way to explaining why the church has been so slow in this area.

However, the number who *have* used social media has doubled in the last five years, so we're never too old to learn. Do you have a smartphone? If not, then your social media options are less varied and less visual, but still entirely accessible.

Age UK is among many organisations doing great work in this area. One of their late-adopter 'digital champions' wrote this:

*Just as not having a phone 20 years ago put people at a disadvantage, not being online is having the same effect today. And society needs older people involved! We have so much wisdom to pass on to the young! You and I know that the spirit of adventure is still very strong in later life! Just because we have*

*creaky knees [it] doesn't mean we don't want to go on
learning and exploring! So go on, give it a try.*[20]

Churches who can put on digital cafés provide an
excellent service to their communities. Resources
like The Bible Reading Fellowship's *The Gift of
Years* programme inspire churches to reach out to
older people.[21] There is nothing whatsoever in the
Bible, no justification, that supports the idea that
we're ever too old to learn. Churches have a unique
opportunity to provide learning opportunities—
particularly in technology—for those more senior.

## 4. Too much hard work?

Church leaders never do all their work for the day.
It takes motivation, *real* motivation, for something
like social media to climb up the internal agenda,
up the mental priority pile, and tip over into actual
action.

If you want to reach younger people but are entirely
invisible on social media, you're simply that much
harder to find. Your building has lost all its signage
and is boarded up. It's about being found. It's
about finding others, and showing them how to be
found by God, in a way that doesn't depend on our
availability.

The hard work sometimes is in thinking through the issues raised by social media. These need to be faced, whether or not you have church profiles, and are examined more closely in the next chapter.

In a Radio 4 *Beyond Belief* discussion in May 2016 on the subject 'Can social media deepen your faith?' it was Muslim Shelina Janmohamed who said this:

*Like any technology it's brought both opportunities and challenges; on the one hand [it's] created spaces for people who might not engage… a new shared identity of being faithful and modern— but on the other hand it's created tensions that need to be resolved. Can you ever represent the depth and transcendental ideas of faith within the small parameters? What happens to the physical congregation? And what about these kinds of new behaviours that really focus around narcissism and celebrity that really are starting to create new challenges for people using it?*[22]

These questions present hard work—hard thinking— for church leaders. They are important to wrestle with. They can't be ignored. You may require one set of expectations, guidelines and boundaries for your personal social media, and another for the community you lead.

As for a church website, if you put the work in now, perhaps someone considering using your church hall will find you online, discover a living breathing body of Christ in their neighbourhood, look into what it means to be a Christian, and encounter God—even while your whole church leadership team are fast asleep in their beds.

## 5. Too unnecessary?

Joan: 'Everyone in our congregation is over 60. Our neighbours are mostly retired. We don't do email or mobiles, or anything like that. We're happy with a news sheet, noticeboard, magazine. That's enough.'

Half of the UK's Anglican churches have fewer than five young people. These churches may not survive into the next generation. Places that have sought to shine a light for the gospel for centuries may have their light extinguished.

If that's you, keep your printed material. It matters. Add on something very simple (next steps in Chapter 3) and play your part in holding out a beacon of light. Play your part in showing the world that the church isn't dead.

Social media might not be necessary for your church but certainly a website is, and, where a website exists, social media may well follow at some stage.

As we've seen, there is nothing inherently bad about the internet, just as there is nothing bad about the concept of newspapers or phones or any other medium. It's possible to use it badly, but, if you use it well, it's a force for good.

A friend of mine had her first novel published and was shocked to discover that her publishers expected to her to become active on Twitter and blogs as part of the publicity contract. It didn't seem necessary. She didn't have a smartphone and readily admitted to being a 'technophobe'. But she gave it a go, and step by step it became unthreatening. Now, as well as helping her book profile enormously, it has brought her a network of like-minded friends in the world of writing, which can otherwise be enormously isolated and isolating.

Read this comment made by a mum in an online forum who was considering church, even though she didn't believe:

*Church brings people together as a village and fosters friendships that wouldn't come about under any other circumstances, typically between people of different ages, classes, etc, all chatting together outside.*[23]

The amazing thing about social media is that it can do all of these things even without a church building.

And it can cost no money at all.

## 6. Too time-consuming?

What is it about social media that takes time? It's not setting up an account or a profile. It's the time it takes to build relationship, and to think about what to communicate—in other words, the things that already take time for churches that are serious about reaching out.

This is the impassioned case on one blog:

*Social media is all or nothing. Either you pour everything you have into it and receive long-term dividends (including growing into a vital and healthy church for the 21st century, reaching lives, building stronger communities and so on), or it will do nothing except reinforce your negativity, your scepticism and your longing for the 'good old days' before the internet. But your presence cannot be in-between. A lukewarm online presence will do more damage for your ministry than no presence at all.*[24]

Perhaps this perspective misses the fact that, certainly for the majority of UK churches, social media will probably never be a full-time role, but it can be an addition to all our communications, a balanced part of the whole. The time that it takes is only time doing what we're already doing, reaching out and building relationships.

It is possible to manage expectations. Most social media tools will give you space for a profile, which can be a useful place to say how often you're likely to post: 'Tweets from the team at St Matthews, every week during term time. The rest of the time you can contact us at…'. Chapter 3 has advice on how to manage this, using scheduling tools and planning how frequently you will post.

There's also the objection that the internet changes too fast. What's the point in spending time learning something that may soon be replaced? Learn one thing and the next is easier. It's incremental, and everyone has to start somewhere.

## 7. Too distracting?

'Humans have a shorter attention span than goldfish, thanks to smartphones' was a headline in *The Telegraph* in March 2016.[25] It's now around eight seconds, based on a study by Microsoft. What is encouraging about this? Here are two suggestions:

- Heavy social media users are focused on identifying what they want and don't want to engage with.
- We are curious, with evidence for an increased craving for information.

What do you think of these in relation to church?

We may 'double screen', checking our phone or tablet while watching television, but arguably the problem of our reduced attention span is offset by our increased hunger for 'content'. And of course, if we're watching our home team lose horribly at football on the television, we can at least be cheered up by the simultaneous comedy commentary on social media.

If you're umbilically attached to your phone, how recently did you try (a) turning it completely off for 24 hours or (b) ignoring it while waiting for a bus or train? Hard, huh?

I was helped recently to read that there are parts of the brain which are only activated when we're completely idle. The spiritual discipline of stillness and contemplation therefore becomes more valuable. Those of you who can't imagine being attached to your phone quite so closely can feel smug about this.

Technology researcher Sherry Turkle gave a TED talk in 2012 in which she said:

*The problem with this new regime of 'I share, therefore I am' is that, if we don't have connection, we don't feel like ourselves. So what do we do? We connect more and more. But in the process, we set ourselves up to be isolated. You end up isolated if you don't cultivate the capacity for solitude, the ability to be separate, to gather yourself. Solitude is where you find yourself so that you can reach out to other people and form real attachments.*[26]

Churches—those hubs of community—can also be places that encourage and facilitate the solitude that leads to real relationship. This is a gift to society! It may seem ironic that social media could drive people to the very context that would help show the value of stillness, of reflection, of focusing on God rather than on the 'cloud of witnesses' around us.

Churches can embody and demonstrate the value of what Sherry Turkle calls 'sacred spaces', where screens are removed for a short time. Part of my effort to be a better parent involves modelling the idea of screen-free 'sacred spaces' at meal times, on the school run, during walks along the seashore or at bedtime.

In the world of 'online content marketing' there are entire courses on how to write a title which will get people clicking out of curiosity and reel them in to consume advertising: it's called 'clickbait' (for those of us with the attention span of goldfish).

You don't need to rise to the bait. You can ignore the stuff you don't care about most easily *if* you know what you're looking for and are aware of the other things you could be doing instead. The fact that social media can be distracting is a reason for reflection and perhaps some self-management, not an excuse not to bother at all.

Tim Chester is one of the Christian thinkers who has written on this subject. He would suggest that the real distraction is the fact that through Facebook (and the point could be extended to other forms of social media) we can recreate our identity to win the approval of others.[27]

Of course it's also true that we can recreate our identity every time we get dressed or rephrase our answer to the frequently dreaded question, 'So, what do you do?'—but social media sometimes requires quick, succinct decisions on how we portray ourselves, which can make us feel uncomfortable.

Our identity as Christians, whether on social media or anywhere else, is in Christ. We're made in the image of God and we claim our identity in Jesus. The theological dimensions of social media are yet another reason to engage thoughtfully with it.

## 8. Too detrimental to mental health?

Churches and those involved in pastoral care need to be aware of the potential effect of social media on mental health. One of many similar studies in 2016 found that one in five adults felt depressed after checking social media.[28] While studies like this always need to be questioned, we know that compulsive screen-flicks, phones in bed, and even just the light from screens can make it harder to sleep. The tendency to base our worth on the attention of others (likes, replies) increases. The rise in body dysmorphia among teenage girls is easy to link to the reflex habit of taking 'selfies'.[29]

On the other hand, remember that for every person who feel that their identity is undermined by social media, there are others who find it a lifeline. I think of my friend who has been housebound for years due to physical and mental illness. Social media has enabled him to sustain friendships, stay on top of what is going on, and draw support from others in a similar situation.

It's hard to give a hug online (even with an emoji), but social media enables us to relate outside of our bodies. For some people, this is a gift from God. Dr Bex Lewis' excellent book *Raising Children in a Digital Age* gives a helpfully balanced perspective on the effect of social media on families and mental health.[30]

Church is a great place to provide guidance and good examples so that young people particularly feel confident in who they are as children of God, whether in church or on Snapchat. The fear of missing out ('FOMO') can remove our ability to be fully present. Even if social media isn't for you personally, support others so that they can use it well.

Jesus saw through people's masks. He communicated face to face. The act of incarnation brought body and spirit together. Social media lends itself to a projection of self—a 'virtual reality' of the perfect life—with smiles, airbrushed pictures and 'curated' content to create the illusion of a chosen identity. Christians are called to be people of integrity. Integrity means being whole, not having one persona in the digital realm and another face to face. Churches and Christians should be the last to be accused of hypocrisy. Be authentic—and take seriously the responsibility of churches to bring people back to their identity in Christ.

## 9. Too hard to sustain?

Starting from nowhere on social media does require a little more than persuasion or even a brief burst of enthusiasm. Actual purpose and determination are useful too! In his excellent book *The Social Church*, Justin Wise describes a scenario we can imagine:

*What started with such promise is now a withered, dry shell of social engagement entropy. People say it doesn't work, which is akin to blaming a shovel for not digging a deep enough hole. It's not the shovel's fault for not digging deep, it's the one wielding the shovel!*[31]

In other words, the people and the plan are key, and so is the connection that social media has to the rest of your existing church communications. This isn't a reason not to bother—it's a reason to plan better (which is what this book will help you to do).

# The summary of why it matters

- If our church doesn't address the reality of social media as a normal communication tool in people's daily lives, a characteristic of our times, we will fail to make the most of the enormous opportunities it presents for outreach and relationships. We will miss out on its theological, behavioural and missional depths.
- If our church doesn't have a social media profile or presence as a community of faith, we might be invisible to those wanting to speak to us.
- If our church has a Facebook page or Twitter account but ignores it, we come across as neglectful at best, rude at worst.
- If our church regularly dips its toe into new social networks and is fully submerged in some, but has forgotten why, or who it's really for, we risk being the 'resounding gong' or 'clanging cymbal' without love (1 Corinthians 13:1).

Social media matters because people matter. People are social, and social media is where people socialise. Jesus moved towards people and entered their crowds. In one crowd, Zacchaeus used a tree to watch Jesus from a distance, to spy on him. Some may have called him a voyeur, but actually he just wanted a friend. How did Jesus respond? He spoke to him, asked him to come down, and the space between them disappeared.

If you suspect that people may be watching you, your church or your faith from a distance on social media, be the one who closes the gap. That way, you may even get invited into people's homes, whether digitally or physically.

In case you're feeling got at—*choose conviction, not accusation!*

It's easy to feel guilty. We feel the accusation of those outside the church: 'You're so behind the times.' We feel the accusation of those within the church: 'We're so behind the times' or perhaps 'We're so missing the point.'

We feel the accusation of our energy levels: 'This is one thing we can do without.' We feel an accusation from this book: 'You should be doing more.'

First, the fact that you picked the book up and have read this far shows that you're doing more than you realise. There's no condemnation here. Those who are working tirelessly in churches, to serve their community and God, deserve support and respect, not further demands. It's not that you *should* be doing more—it's that you *can* take the next step with vision, motivation, purpose, even excitement.

The Bible describes the devil as 'the accuser of our brothers and sisters, who accuses them… day and night' (Revelation 12:10). Satan actually means 'accuser'. Accusation leads to defensiveness and passivity—not to action. It's not the voice of God.

One of the most liberating truths I was ever taught was the difference between conviction and condemnation. 'There is now no condemnation'—*no condemnation!*—'for those who are in Christ Jesus' (Romans 8:1). When I feel condemned, it's not from God. When I feel convicted, however, it can be the power of the Holy Spirit, calling me to action and probably to repentance. 'Dear children, let us not love with words or speech but with actions and in truth,' says 1 John 3:18.

When we communicate as a church, in action, in truth, it is an act of love.

In one of his last pieces of communication before he officially retired, Pope Benedict XVI put it this way:

*The digital environment is not a parallel or purely virtual world, but is part of the daily experience of many people, especially the young. Social networks are the result of human interaction, but for their part they also reshape the dynamics of communication which builds relationships: a considered understanding of this environment is therefore a prerequisite for a significant presence there.*[32]

The fight for people's attention grows.

You don't need to do much to stay in the sight lines of those looking for you. What you *can't* do is be invisible.

It doesn't take much—not really. Not in the context of a year. Not in the light of eternity.

All you need is a plan.

# 2

# What to consider first

Before you set out to create or overhaul your church plan to incorporate social media, there are five strategic questions that can form the foundation of a long-term plan.

When someone asks you if you've 'really thought this through', you want to be able to say yes! You could use these questions with a group.

- What is our current reality?
- What is the core message we're communicating?
- Who is our focus?
- Can we communicate an identity that is cohesive, consistent and credible?
- Are our expectations realistic and shared with the church?

## What is our current reality?

If you don't yet have a church website, it is excellent that you are reading this book, but you may want to look at *Church Online: Websites* in this series. It asks the questions you'll need to address in order to start developing a church digital presence.

Some churches have a Facebook page instead of a website, usually because it is familiar and free. This can work for some groups, but you'll always be heavily restricted by the way it looks and what it can do. Also, it excludes people who aren't on Facebook from participating, so perhaps it's not a good long-term strategy.

If you have tried various social media platforms in the past but they've been neglected or abandoned, don't brush the issue under the carpet. What are the reasons for the neglect? Are any of these media likely to resurface if you give it another shot?

Don't jump too quickly to blame an individual. If the vision is strong enough, and if social media is embedded into the broader context of your church communications, then good planning can prevent the responsibility from falling on one person.[33]

If your church is active on social media but perhaps occasionally forgets why, you could benefit from a careful 'point in time' evaluation.

Analytics—the data provided by most social networks on how many people you're reaching, what they're checking and when—can be really useful as a marker in time to track changes, and as a cool, calm, quantitative evaluation or report. Have you taken time to read through the balance of your posts, replies and engagements?

Ask the questions, 'What was the purpose of this piece of communication? Was it effective? Did it engage people?' If you put events on Facebook, do people respond? Do you ever encourage them to do so from the front of church? Do you use email or print, your news sheet or magazine, to encourage social media use in the church?

Ultimately your social media strategy needs to start with a bigger look at all of your church communications, digitally, outside the church (your building and invitations) and inside (your welcome and publications). The other books in this series will be helpful here.

First, identify where you want to develop and grow as a church. This is the current reality that matters for your communications. Then use digital tools to support your growth.

# What is the core message we're communicating?

If you're discussing this as a team, ask the question (even if it sounds like management-speak): what would 'success' look like for our church social media? Would it be someone coming to church for the first time? Someone growing in their faith at home? Or the community being better connected? You can aim to do all three, of course—but the core message you're communicating will differ, depending on which is your priority.

Here's another question: are you pushing or are you pulling? Websites traditionally 'push' their message out. They declare. They explain. Social media is better placed to pull people in, with content that is relevant, interesting or intriguing—and then to start a two-way conversation that builds relationship.

In Jeremiah 31:3, God says, 'I have drawn you with loving-kindness' (NIV 1984). What would it look like if our church digital strategy were to draw people in with loving-kindness?

Social media is not just a place to broadcast a message. Of course, churches want to preach a message, but social media is also a place to be social. In church service terms, it's more like the coffee time than the notices; more like the sign-up sheet than the preaching. It enables dialogue.

The blog ChurchTechToday puts it like this:

*Throwing our message 'out there' into the digital space without hanging around for the conversation (and maybe even joining conversations that are not our own), makes people want to block us. It's that simple.*[34]

Large companies have had to learn this lesson. According to one report, more than 93% of the tweets sent by the 20 biggest companies in the world were personal messages to individuals.[35] Social media is a way for faceless corporations to acquire a face. They're applying the marketing mantra 'Attract—Convert—Close—Delight', with the emphasis on 'delight'. One marketer gave this advice to companies:

*Responses need to be on-brand, in the right tone and voice, and fast. Don't just stop at answering questions. Try to make the most of these valuable customer touch points with an arsenal of assets (like coupon codes) to make your 1:1 marketing strategy stick, and get those customers talking about your brand in the best way possible.*[36]

A UK church considering its core message can take something even from this classic piece of marketing blurb.

- If your primary aim is connectedness, fellowship, relationships, then ensure you have a person who will respond.

- Sometimes respond with questions as well as answers.

- Address people by name, with the language you'd use if you were speaking in person.

- Encourage photo sharing from the congregation and explain the ability of social media to do this (but take great care with photos of children and young people—see the advice later under the heading 'Don't promote sin').

- If you want to set targets for the time you invest in social media, think carefully as a group about how you will measure results, and whether your core message is about pushing church or pulling others to Christ.

## Who is our focus?

When you're considering which tool is best for which audience, think about how Jesus contextualised his communication for his audience. He knew whether each person was preoccupied with sheep or corn or religion, and he met them at that point.

He knew how to tell a story that suited the context, whether it was a crowd or an intimate gathering. Jesus spoke to emotion, not logic, knowing that this would strengthen people's memories of what they heard. Searching questions, metaphors, powerful images… these were the ways that Jesus communicated to the curious, to the willing and to those whose ears were closed against him.

Perhaps your church is exploring social media because, like so many churches in the UK, you want to attract 'young families'. Perhaps you know that churches with young people are twice as likely to be flourishing, and you want young people to hear about Jesus.[37]

Dig into the question of whether the people you want to reach are on Facebook, Twitter, Instagram, or perhaps none of these—in which case (and this may sound obvious) there may be a better way to reach them than through social media!

One church in Eastbourne set up a Twitter account because they felt they should. No one in the church is on Twitter—so they're now considering using it solely to attract students and to connect with local businesses that want to use the hall. That's focus.

Another church had a Facebook page for events, which was rarely used. The big community youth group, however, were really active on Instagram—so the church ditched Facebook altogether. They did a survey to find out what their members used, so that anything the church created on social media could be shared by members with their friends. It would be 'likeable' and 'shareable'.

Asking 'Who is this really for?' will prevent you from wasting time on something that has no focus or purpose. It might also give you a necessary excuse not to indulge the enthusiasms of one person, if these are not closely connected to the identity and mission of the church.

## Can we communicate an identity that is cohesive, consistent and credible?

All our church communications should fit together, each with their own character but obviously from the same community. Our credibility rests more than we realise on our consistency. When a person demonstrates consistency, we're less likely to think they're a hypocrite. When a church consistently communicates with the same personality, we are more likely to think it has integrity.

Imagine if a church social media stream looked like this on three consecutive weeks:

- Will you be there on Sunday?? It'll be soooo fun!!! ;-) ;-)
- This Sunday. Service 10.30 am. All welcome.
- Live in New Village? Free on Sunday? Why not try your local church? 10.30 am, free kids' activities and refreshments. Just turn up. [website]

Have you ever read the sides of an Innocent smoothie carton? That's a company 'voice', a tone, a writing style, consistent on every 'channel'. Churches, of course, are groups of people. We probably don't have a set of brand guidelines, let alone any rules extending to tone of language. This means we need to be a bit more self-aware.

The tone we might use with our best friends or family in a private WhatsApp group probably isn't appropriate when representing the church. Neither is the tone we'd use in an email to a solicitor. Speak as you'd speak in person, to someone you wanted to welcome. You may need to meet as a group to establish the tone of voice that best matches who you are in person. In fact, this might prove to be a really interesting conversation. What is the character of your church? How do you talk? How do you want to talk?

If someone knows your church only through Facebook, they'll want that message to be consistent with what they encounter in person. It points to integrity. It engenders trust. This is yet another reason why social media needs to fit with your whole communications strategy. If it's cohesive, it's more credible. But of course it first requires that you know your identity—even down to how that sounds when read through a Facebook or Twitter post.

## Do we have guidelines to create shared expectations?

Before I give some positive examples of tried-and-tested guidelines for social media use, there are some pitfalls to avoid. Gervase Markham from Sheffield describes in *Evangelicals Now*[38] some times when sharing isn't caring.

## Don't attack people

It's a simple cycle: someone says or does something stupid, thoughtless, or both. With a sense of righteous indignation you find yourself part of the baying mob, and occasionally lives are devastated by it.[39] When your gut tells you that what you're posting or sharing may be controversial—when you find yourself hesitating even for a split second—ask yourself what would happen if someone who really disliked you (or really respected you) read it. Proverbs 17:9 says: 'Whoever would foster love covers over an offence, but whoever repeats the matter separates close friends.'

## Don't spread lies

Sometimes what we read on the internet isn't even true. Gervase Markham writes:

*'A lie will go round the world while truth is pulling its boots on.'*

*The first search hit for the above quote attributes it to Mark Twain, the second to Winston Churchill. And this neatly illustrates the accuracy problem. Many items shared on social media are designed to shock, to cause outrage, or to confirm our political views or our opinions of others. Sharing such things with*

*like-minded friends shows them we are on the side
of good (this phenomenon now has a name—'virtue
signalling'). But for that reason this is also the content
we are least suspicious of. How can it be wrong? I
agree with it!*

*However, it turns out that much or most of it is,
on closer examination, misleading, partly wrong or
entirely false.*

If you're not sure, don't rush to agree.

## Don't spread rubbish

Churches are unlikely to do this on purpose, you'd
hope! But as individuals it's easy to sink into the
funny silly stuff, and accidentally become oblivious
to the sordid heart of it all.

In 2012 I went to Ethiopia for a couple of months.
Internet access was limited, so I saved it for updating
a Tumblr blog for friends and family (password
protected—my kids were too young to have their
adventures shared with the world). I had no TV, no
newspapers, no social media.

After a month we had visitors from the UK, bringing
the Sunday papers from their flight. My reaction to
the contents of those papers was unexpected. I'd
had a month without any fashion journalism and

its gratuitous exposure, without any voyeuristic crime stories or grim articles on violence and porn and abuse. Normally I read piles of papers at the weekend and consider myself fairly unshockable, but this felt dirty, like an unpleasant intrusion into the simple life we'd been enjoying.

I realised how numb I'd become to reading words that elevated greed and pain rather than truth and goodness. Titillated by tat—let's not do it.

How about this as a shared expectation within our church for social media?

*Devote yourselves to prayer, being watchful and thankful. And pray for us, too, that God may open a door for our message, so that we may proclaim the mystery of Christ, for which I am in chains. Pray that I may proclaim it clearly, as I should. Be wise in the way you act toward outsiders; make the most of every opportunity. Let your conversation be always full of grace, seasoned with salt, so that you may know how to answer everyone.* (Colossians 4:2–6)

Most church networks now publish guidelines on social media. Links are in Chapter 4 (including one set which made national news for its level of practical advice, despite the Diocese of Bath and Wells' concession that it was 'worthy but a bit on the dull side'!).

Some churches have particular guidelines for the use of social media, and Snapchat in particular, with young people. The Child Exploitation and Online Protection Centre has produced www.thinkuknow.co.uk, which gives important guidelines. Adults working in churches are advised not to initiate contact with children, young people or vulnerable adults on social media, or to have private conversations.

When you're putting together guidelines for your church, make sure you define 'social media' as explicitly as you need, remind people why guidelines are necessary, and remind people why you're using social media in the first place—where it fits in your communication as a whole. The lists below are a summary, drawn from many churches' guidelines.

These social media pointers could apply to any individual or organisation:

- Your posting is permanent. Even if you delete it, it may have been seen and stored.[40]
- You don't need to reply quickly.
- Don't be anonymous.

- Use privacy settings wisely. Don't give home addresses or phone numbers.
- Don't get hacked: make passwords long, varied and complicated, and use up-to-date security software and firewalls.
- Ignore potential spam links or requests from strangers.
- Ask yourself: would I be happy with God / my mum / my children reading this?
- Would you be happy to publish your message more widely?
- If you're sharing a post, do you have permission to do so? Does the copyright belong to the creator or to someone else who requires payment or needs to give permission?
- Is your message lifting others up or pushing them down?

Now add these, which are specifically relevant to churches and church leaders:

- If your social media account has the church logo, website or address, avoid expressing personal opinions on it.
- If church leaders are on social media, are they there in an entirely personal capacity or with the same awareness of their professional role

as they'd have on a Sunday morning? It's not necessarily easy to draw the line, but people contacting their church leader on social media, particularly about pastoral issues, may find it helpful if the distinction between personal and professional is made clear.

- If inappropriate or pastoral information starts to be shared, take the conversation out of social media. If sharing pastoral information feels like gossip (or, in fact, is gossip), don't do it.

- Information from a closed or confidential group or meeting should be kept within that group.

- Safeguarding: don't include pictures of children, communicate directly with children or add them as friends to your personal social networking page. Behave as you would publicly, with appropriate safeguarding measures and policies in place. Churches need to be above reproach in this area, for obvious legal and pastoral reasons.

- Ask yourself: am I being a good representative of the church?

- If you link to a website, this could be seen as an endorsement of its content. Are you happy to publicise and promote it?

# What advice does the Bible give?

A Bible study on some pertinent verses can really help a group wanting to dig into a deeper perspective on social media. Here are some suggestions to whet your appetite, and there are questions for small-group discussion in Chapter 4 (Toolkit).

- Proverbs 15:23
- Proverbs 18:2
- Proverbs 29:11
- Matthew 5:16
- Matthew 15:10–20
- Matthew 22:39
- Mark 12:28–31
- Acts 20:28
- 1 Corinthians 6:12
- Philippians 2:3
- Philippians 2:14–16
- 1 Thessalonians 5:10–11

# 3

# Essential next steps

## Choose your tools

Online you'll find every social media introduction and masterclass you could ever need: just type 'How to get started on Facebook / Instagram / Twitter' into YouTube.

Research in 2016 found that Christians are more likely to use Facebook for faith-related social media posts than other tools—and that over 70% often or sometimes link to a church or Christian charity.[41]

Of course, by the time you read this, there may be other platforms to consider. Video and livestreaming is the biggest area of growth. Even in 2016, a survey found that 20% of those surveyed often or sometimes livestreamed Christian meetings[42]—and this figure looks set to grow. Talitha Proud, from Church of England digital communications, suggests that this offers 'real opportunity for churches to reach more people in a completely new way, revealing not just what their Sunday service looks like but how the church is part of the local community seven days a week'.[43] There is more on this and other tools in this chapter.

The handy guide on the following pages suggests the conversation you might have with someone in your church about different platforms. It's a basic introduction, with just enough detail to encourage them to be used.

# Facebook 

### *That's the one where...*

- we look at photos from everyone we've lost touch with (and try not to be jealous).
- Facebook Messenger, groups, chat, video and events enable people to plan their social lives and stay in touch.

### *Seems to be particularly popular with...*

- parents, church groups, brands.
- everyone I really ought to see sometime.

### *Churches often use it for...*

- publicising events and finding out who is coming.
- creating community both within and outside the church.

### *And if you want to go further...*

- set up private groups for smaller pastoral or study groups, where you can share prayer requests, news, ministry opportunities, links and resources that add to what you're studying.
- use Facebook Live to livestream a message or event. Make it less than five minutes, with a great description, clear purpose and lots of personality.

# Twitter 🐦

### That's the one where…

- you post really short messages with hashtags (for example, #prayforparis) and internet links.
- the tweets from those you 'follow' create a never-ending stream of headlines from your own personally curated newspaper.

### Seems to be particularly popular with…

- politicians, journalists, celebrities, bloggers and enthusiasts.
- trolls, extremists and rabble rousers.

### Churches could use it for…

- short inspiration or links to blogs and audio.
- announcements, reminders and invitations.
- focusing on local areas of interest, community activities or photos.

### And if you want to go further…

- stream a live service using Periscope.
- join in with or even initiate a planned public conversation with a dedicated hashtag on a chosen issue. If everyone is talking about #joytotheworld, join in! If you use the hashtag, people searching for it will find your comment.

# YouTube ▶

### *That's the one where…*
- many under-30s 'consume' visual media as an alternative to TV.
- the videos cover everything you can imagine, the adverts are increasingly ubiquitous and the comments best avoided.

### *Seems to be particularly popular with…*
- video bloggers (vloggers), performers, their audience, pranksters and comedy cat fans.
- people with a skill to share—everything from 'how to fix your boiler' to 'how to pray'.

### *Churches could use it for…*
- short videos (two minutes max) interviewing people in the church or community, showing photos, encouraging giving or telling a story.
- showing or sharing excellent outreach content produced by many organisations, particularly around Christmas, Halloween and Easter.

### *And if you want to go further…*
- record interviews as chat using Blab or similar, and upload on to your dedicated channel.
- stream a live service.
- also use Vimeo to make your films downloadable.

# WhatsApp 📱

## *That's the one where...*

- you create a group from people's mobile numbers and can send them a message all in one go—group text, basically, but exclusive to smartphones and free to send and receive over the internet.
- everything is encrypted and can be seen only by people in the group—private, not public.

## *Seems to be particularly popular with...*

- groups of friends sharing news, photos, videos or prayer requests.
- the 'designated event organiser', trying to tell everyone what the logistical plan is for the much anticipated get-together.

## *Churches could use it for...*

- small-group prayer requests and news.
- short-term event planning, without endless email threads.

## *And if you want to go further...*

- create an 'I need / I can offer' community group.
- record short audio or video messages to send to a group—you can have up to 50,000 subscribers to one number.[44]

# Pinterest

### *That's the one where…*

- you 'pin' an image or website, with a caption, on to a themed board, like a scrapbook, and follow others that you like.
- there are lots of boards focused on weddings, recipes, holidays and fashion—and a large number with 'scripture art' or 'inspirational quotes'.

### *Seems to be particularly popular with…*

- women looking for creative inspiration.
- event planners, particularly brides-to-be.

### *Churches could use it for…*

- sharing fabulous displays or publicity examples to inspire others.
- locally focused collections of images or links as marketing—just include your location in your profile and in every single pin.

### *And if you want to go further…*

- create recommended resources and inspiration boards for ministry groups.
- set up an 'ideas board' for Christmas, Easter or Messy Church.

# Snapchat

### *That's the one where…*

- photos ('snaps') usually disappear after a set time (unless saved as 'memories').
- you can add filters, stickers, captions and annotations to photos (the filters can make you look very strange).

### *Seems to be particularly popular with…*

- everyone under the age of 25.
- companies investing in social media/youth.

### *Churches could use it for…*

- quick reminders of events.
- a photo-diary 'day in the life' of church leaders, charities or projects—or, as Snapchat would call it, a 'story'.
- encouraging community among young people.

### *And if you want to go further…*

- teach your young people about safe use of Snapchat and the themes it raises of temporary/eternal, appearance, identity and so on.
- create a 'story' of a church event, from planning and set-up to packing away.

# LinkedIn 💼

### *That's the one where…*

- people put their CVs online and build business connections.
- companies and freelancers write articles and initiate work-related discussions.

### *Seems to be particularly popular with…*

- anyone looking for a job.
- anyone looking for new employees.

### *Churches could use it for…*

- a short church 'company page' with links to the website.
- encouraging people in the church to connect with each other and join their work lives with their church life, with huge potential fruit.

### *And if you want to go further…*

- look for others in your area who share a passion for work in the community.
- look at the skills and experiences of your congregation to see where they could contribute.
- consider posting blog content as LinkedIn posts to reach other communities.

## Google Plus G+

***That's the one where…***

- people form circles of contacts—similar to Facebook.
- you get signed up when you get a free Gmail email account.

***Seems to be particularly popular with…***

- people working for Google.
- people covering all their social media bases.

***Churches could use it for…***

- increasing their SEO (Search Engine Optimisation), as Google+ pages appear high in Google rankings.

***And if you want to go further…***

- promote it for encouraging shared content—for example, alongside Google Docs and Google Drive.
- create posts which will not be filtered from its users (as they would be on Facebook) and are designed to appear on Google searches, with a higher chance of engagement from followers.

When choosing the best tool, go back to the questions we asked in Chapter 2: 'What is the core message we're communicating?' and 'Who is our focus?'

Suppose your focus is on people already connected to the church, to strengthen community among them. If they're on Facebook more than any other social media platform, use this. One church in Hove set up a Facebook group for anyone, from any church, who was interested in praying for one particular neighbourhood. It grew to hundreds of people within days.

If your core message is about opening up your services as broadly as possible, or if you are keen to experiment, consider learning from the ChurchLive project and livestream a service. Here are some comments from those who've tried:

*The technology was easy and cheap to set up. Clearly, people connected with it. We're considering streaming our daily prayer service to enable those who can't come in person to join in from work or home.*

*St Andrews is a church that's keen to reach out via every channel possible. It's crucial to be part of the social media world and reach out on new platforms.*

*To be broadcasting to so many people from a small mobile is an incredible opportunity.*

*Our congregation numbers vary significantly, and livestreaming will open up new avenues for members to join us when they can't travel, and for weddings and baptisms to be joined from across the world. We very much look forward to seeing how this changes our outreach and how it may shape our liturgical mission in the future.*

When you stream a service, you don't necessarily get the reward of seeing 'bums on pews', faces, comments or smiles. It requires trust that God is using and even multiplying your efforts. This is true of much social media. It returns us to the mindset of faithful outreach and service, where, to use the old saying, 'the results department is God's department'.

We don't do it for the likes. We do it for the love of God.

Very practically, here are six pieces of advice from the Archbishops' Council Digital Media Officer, on broadcasting from church. Some of these tips could helpfully be applied to other social media tools too.

- Choose the right platform. For broadcasting it might be Periscope, Facebook Live or YouTube.

- Name your broadcast (or profile) so that people who stumble across it know what it is.
- Promote your broadcast in advance so that people know when to look out for it. (This is good advice for any social media you launch. Tell people about it in other ways—by word of mouth, email, or even by post if necessary.)
- Confirm that you have the right music / performer licences to broadcast. (See Chapter 4: Toolkit for advice on copyright.)
- Check with your safeguarding officer or vicar if you're filming children.
- Experiment with camera setup and location to find the best place for filming, and be creative.[45]

Here are some examples of creative uses of different social media tools from around the UK church, all shortlisted for awards in 2015/2016, and how the ideas could be applied to local churches:

- **Video:** tgimonday.show from the Diocese of Lichfield broadcasts regular 'episodes' in which a panel of five people answer questions from the public about Christianity. Could local churches film short two-way interviews with visitors to the church?

- **Twitter:** #josephtweets from Messy Church, a fun idea telling the Christmas story through the eyes of Joseph in daily bite-size chunks. Could local churches retweet ideas like this or create a local event hashtag with daily updates (#morecambechristmas)? #FatherKevinprays or similar could be a good way to pull together prayers, sayings or tweets from a well-loved local vicar.

- **Facebook:** St Mary Bredin, Canterbury, is one example of a church with a successful website and a Facebook page to match, at facebook.com/smbcanterbury. It contains a solid mix of photos of activities and community, event publicity, videos and printed publicity. Quotes as images, pictures of people having fun, countdowns to events, prayer requests and links to blogs are all useful ingredients for an active Facebook presence.

- **Instagram:** A collage of church in action, inspiring words, events and stories about wider relationships (such as international connections)—this is what Instagram can achieve so beautifully. St Thomas Norwich (@stnchurch) is one church that makes their posts consistent, regular and people-focused, demonstrating genuine community.

- **Snapchat:** Harder work for churches, but the fastest growing of them all, Snapchat is as current as it gets. As one writer puts it, 'It's encouraging a new generation of social media users to live in the moment. Forget about curating a flawless feed of your life [of] what happened yesterday. Just focus on right now.'[46] Churches that use Snapchat focus it on one person—probably the leader —with frequent candid posts, no scheduling, no newsfeeds and no history (unless certain snaps are saved as 'memories'). It can enhance community among students and youth, and a story shared with everyone who has 'added' you can have a wide reach.

For content ideas, many of them relevant to any form of social media, read on.

## Choose your look

Choosing a 'look' for your church social media account is easier than for your website. One can reflect the other. Upload a really simple background image or pattern as your header, then put your logo on top. The ideal size for social media banners and headers sometimes changes, but tools like those listed under 'Tools for creating social media graphics' in Chapter 4 (Toolkit) can help you create exactly the right size.

A simple logo is fine as your profile image. Some churches add extra features to support campaigns (sometimes called 'twibbons')—for example, the symbol ن was used by many people to express solidarity with persecuted Christians in the Middle East, who had the symbol daubed on their doors. It is the Arabic letter 'N', short for 'Nasrani', which means 'Christian'.

You will need to create a summary or description for the profile page of some accounts. This is an opportunity to give more information than just your name. Include your location and contact details.

Use keywords that are accurate and true to your community—your village, town or city, your name and probably your denomination or church network. Then think about the kind of words people type into Google when they're looking for a church: friendly, local, school, building, community, children, youth, activities, international, historic, vibrant, all ages, peaceful, inclusive, spiritual, traditional, CofE, Alpha, services, information, parish, nearby.[47]

Link to your website and all your other social media accounts in your profile.

Remember, you can show the congregation how everything looks, either in print or onscreen in a service, whether they are on social media or not.

# Plan your year

Depending on your target audience for each social media tool, first think about a rhythm of mission throughout the year—the key times of focus, such as Christmas, Easter or the big week of prayer.

- **Focus on a tool**—for example, a Facebook group.
- **Who's your target?** It might be the parent and toddler group, or local community groups.
- **What are the peak times?** It might be Christmas, Easter or a holiday club. These are the times to plan your posts carefully.
- **At normal times, how frequently can you post?** It might be weekly, at the same time as doing the news sheet, or a quick message every morning.

## Ways to make it happen

- Schedule in advance so that posts appear automatically when you want them to (see Chapter 4: Toolkit). The only risk with this method is that your jokey Tweet or Facebook post, planned months ago, may unfortunately coincide with a tragedy in the news, and you'll appear grossly insensitive simply by being organised. If you needed a reason to have your phone alert you to breaking news, this is it! You can always postpone or cancel your scheduled posts—or just take the risk.

- Create posts, share, take photos, film or tweet at the same time as something else that happens in the church calendar—even if it's just comments on the sermon during the sermon. This way, the calendar event will act as a natural trigger.

- Have one person you trust who can post from their phone when they feel like it.

- Don't always post at the same time of day, and feel free to mix the live with the scheduled (impossible on Snapchat).

- Have a designated person who will respond to any direct messages, because to ignore contact on social media is just as rude as ignoring someone at the door of the church. It doesn't always need to be the same person. Read more on this in 'Find your team'.

# Find your content

Every piece of research confirms what our finger reflexes already tell us: the most popular content is always video or photos. This can seem daunting, particularly for church leaders who are more adept with sermons and the proclamation of the word rather than the image.

Images create questions, tell stories and affirm community.

Smartphones make it very simple to take photos and film videos, potentially very good ones, and share them instantly. Events, volunteers, smiling faces, cups of tea brewed, cakes baked, crafts constructed, and even the church building—all are rich and easily found material. You don't need to prerecord. You can now stream video live on most platforms, which will often be accessible at a later stage too.

Take some words, perhaps a quote or line from a song, and create an image out of them using an app like those listed in Chapter 4 (Toolkit).

Read your Bible on an app like YouVersion and create an image out of your favourite verse to share on social media. My daughter loves this. It has enriched her Bible reading and enabled her to dwell on verses without even realising that she's memorising them at the same time.

Commission your children, youth group or holiday club to make a video—perhaps a drama, a song, or a speeded-up film of them constructing something or playing a game. They'll love it. The church will love it. Just make sure you get the parents' permission first.

Film the church leader saying exactly what they'd say from the front, on any subject. YouTube has some amazing examples of straight sermons turned into something watchable with clever 'kinetic typography' (a fun project for someone techy, perhaps), or just some background music or photos over the top. Very possibly, the young people in your church are taught how to use iMovie or other video editing software at school. Ask them. Perhaps they could have a go.

Ask missionaries you support to film a short 'hello and thank you' or a tour around their house and area. This is far easier to achieve than a visit in person and could be hugely inspiring. Just don't forget to be extremely careful if your missionaries work in a sensitive area or ministry. Don't name people or the countries they work in, if it is likely to endanger them or their work. This sort of information should never

ever be on a church website, even on password-protected pages.

Finally, you can always post material by organisations you trust, authors you respect, theologians you value, your church network or your denomination. Promote the work of other churches in your area too. It honours God, it builds fellowship, and the Bible tells us clearly that our love for one another speaks louder than any image or video.

For any church members mindlessly scrolling through baby pictures, holiday snaps and politics on Facebook at 4.00 pm on a Wednesday afternoon, something out of the blue that points them to God could be exactly what they need. The number following Christian organisations online is double those following their own pastor or minister, but analysis has confirmed that 'diversity is the recommended order of the day—a mix of textual, image-based and audio / video content, posted regularly so that grassroots believers can easily find it and share it among their own circle of influence'.[48]

Don't be tempted only to post Bible verses. For a start, you may be taking them entirely out of context. Also, a study in 2015 found that about half of the Bible verses tweeted that year were sent automatically, by robots. 'Bible spam' isn't a great advertisement for the efficacy of social media.[49]

If you have a particularly important event or a post that explains better than anything else who you are, you can 'pin' posts to the top of your Facebook or Twitter page so that they always appear first. There are time limits on Facebook for how long you can pin a post, but not on Twitter.

If you search online for 'churches making the most of Facebook' or 'best church uses of Twitter' you'll find more ideas than you can use. I guarantee that they'll almost all be from the USA, so you may need to translate them into a UK context. If you're only interested to see UK results, click on 'Search tools' when you see the result and change 'Any country' to 'Country: the UK'. You can take inspiration from non-church organisations too. Just google 'social media content ideas'.

There is also a list of starter post ideas in Chapter 4 (Toolkit)—a list of 'ingredients' that you can tailor for the recipe most appropriate to your community and your tool.

Hashtags on Twitter and Instagram can enable individuals and churches quickly to join a broader conversation. Click on a hashtag to see others commenting on the same current theme. Some examples, if you're a starter, are #40acts, #prayforsyria and #bbcqt. If there is a large Christian conference you wish you were at, search for the hashtag and see photos, comments, even summaries of sessions. For example, searching for #PremDAC16 will give you a flavour of the Premier Digital Media Conference in November 2016, which was all about equipping churches to reach out through digital media.

Some churches even have signs in church that encourage social media use or give a public Wi-Fi code, perhaps with suggested places where people can 'live tweet' their services out of view.

A final word: before a 'peak time'—Christmas, Easter, Harvest, Remembrance, a holiday club or significant service—do everything you can to make sure your social media matches the rest of your church communications. If you've created a poster for outside the church, use the same image for social media, even if that just means taking a photo of the poster. If you have an invitation, make it look the same. Consistency is very achievable, highly beneficial, but easily neglected.

# Find your team

Large companies regularly employ someone from outside to manage their social media. Some celebrities readily confess to not writing their own tweets. Adele has admitted that she has to go through two levels of management before pressing 'send'. In 2014 the *Huffington Post* explained that 'typically, celebs hire ghost Twitterers to avoid unnecessary press, maintain their brand, and keep to their busy schedules'.[50]

Do churches share the same issues as celebs? Of course! 'Avoid unnecessary press'—ask the Church of England. 'Maintain their brand'—yes, even if we don't always use that exact phrase. 'Keep to busy schedules'—absolutely, albeit as a result of working with volunteers rather than going on world tours.

But churches can't have social media run by 'ghost' people who don't know the vision of the church or what is going on in it. The first and most important qualification for someone doing your social media is that they understand your church.

They also need to be wise enough to avoid un-necessary and distracting controversy (particularly of the political or theological kind, unless you're intentionally trying to provoke 'robust debate'). A church social media presence is not the place for one 'editor' to push their personal agenda.

Your social media person needs to be 'on message', maintaining the brand, in the sense that what they post must be consistent with who you are as a church. Being 'on brand' is about integrity, honesty and truthfulness. A supercool Instagram feed won't fit with every community.

They need to have a schedule or at least have worked out how social media can fit in with the busyness of everything else they do. A Facebook page that's not updated for three years is just as bad as an out-of-date website, and probably worse than not having one at all.

Someone who is already active with a particular tool is ideal to take charge of your social media, because they won't need to learn. More importantly, checking and posting will already be ingrained into their habits, so adding another account to the mix won't necessarily prove onerous.

But it's not essential to have an 'expert'. One of the reasons social media is growing in popularity is that it is so very easy to learn. You could start by setting up an account for a small group from church, rather than for the whole church, just to have a go.

Your designated people don't need to be young, trendy or techy, but they do need to be willing to learn, curious, discerning and wise.

Finally, don't talk about social media just on social media. Talk about it in your magazine, from the front of church, in a sermon and at events. Show the church what your social media pages look like on a screen if you can, even if many in the congregation are not on the internet. This will help people to catch a vision and could reduce, not increase, the likelihood that anyone will feel excluded.

To increase your visibility, put social media icons prominently on your website and your printed materials. Actively make connections with people, don't just wait for them to happen.

Encourage people who are active on Facebook, Twitter or Instagram to talk about how God is at work through it. Encourage them to tell stories of what they are learning. You might take a group from your church to the Premier Digital Media conference[51] or ask a young person to lead a session showing the most inspiring things they've found on Instagram.

Perhaps you've read this far and are unconvinced that a social media presence for your church is what you need right now. That's OK—but, to reach out to our communities, we need at least to be informed, stay informed and be open to what God is doing— and to what he might call us to do. If you do what you've always done, you'll get what you've always got. Is it time to step out of what is comfortable, go to where people are and see what happens?

As Christians we're called to 'spur one another on towards love and good deeds' (Hebrews 10:24). Even if some social media tools aren't your thing, encourage others, engage, stay informed and see the potential.

To keep up to date, use the 'Toolkit' provided in Chapter 4, and find more links and resources at cpo. org.uk/toolkit.

# 4

# Toolkit

For a current overview of popular articles on churches and social media, go to www.buzzsumo.com and type 'church social media' into the search bar. If you google your preferred tool, the word 'church' and year (for example, Facebook church 2017), you will be inundated with excellent current advice.

Here are some starters for 2017. All these links and more can be found at cpo.org.uk/toolkit. Where you see 'bit.ly', it is a shortcut link to type in.

## Social media church guidelines

Search for 'church social media guidelines' and the following:

- 'Diocese of York', particularly the points on 'Being a high profile individual on social media'.
- 'Bath and Wells', especially for some great action points from Steve Tilley for those considering dipping a toe into social media for the first time: bit.ly/BathWells.

- 'Diocese of Lichfield', with guidance on clergy relationships, and PCC guidelines on social media and young people.

These guidelines could all be usefully applied to churches of other denominations.

## Social media, children and young people's resources

The Methodist Church guidelines have been carefully considered: bit.ly/Methodistguidelines.

Those working with children and young people should also familiarise themselves with www. thinkuknow.co.uk. There are sections designed for each age group, for parents and for teachers and trainers (Sunday school teachers and youth workers).

For more, I suggest the excellent book by Bex Lewis, *Raising Children in a Digital Age* (Lion, 2014), which has a very handy 'jargon buster' and bibliography.

## Questions for small-group discussion on social media

The following questions are suggested by Thom Rainer (www.smallgroups.com).

- How do you use social media? If you don't use social media, why not?
- How have you seen social media used for good? How have you seen it used for harm?
- How can social media 'magnify our voices in unprecedented ways'?
- When have you been tempted to share a 'retouched' version of your life on social media? What is the effect of sharing a not-completely-accurate portrayal of your life?
- How does your social media usage affect your face-to-face relationships?
- What guidelines do you think Christians should use when they post, tweet or pin?

## UK church communications blogs

- www.churchtrain.uk
- www.premierdigital.org.uk
- www.samevine.co.uk/blog
- www.churchesaliveonline.com/blog

Church website and administration providers such as Church123, ChurchEdit, ChurchApp and ChurchBox also provide blog and training content.

## US church communications blogs

- www.churchtechtoday.com
- www.churchmarketingsucks.com
- www.churchm.ag
- www.thecreativepastor.com
- www.churchjuice.com
- www.prochurchtools.com

You can sign up for updates from these blogs. If the quantity of information is overwhelming, schedule a time to review, or stick to the most relevant one.

## Church advice for various platforms (examples)

- Snapchat: bit.ly/2e5Pd76 from ProChurchTools
- Twitter: bit.ly/2fjLnr2 from ChurchTechToday
- Instagram: bit.ly/1LIryxP from Steve Fogg
- Facebook Live: bit.ly/2f8DjX5 from Katie Allred

# Ideas for posts

- A quote from a Sunday talk, maybe with a picture as background
- Bible verses, perhaps with images from VerseFirst or YouVersion apps
- Questions, especially if real and not rhetorical
- Behind-the-scenes photos of events or even of the church office
- 'Meet the team' profiles and pictures
- Thanks and recognition for volunteers
- Devotional thoughts
- Quotes from great writers (there are Twitter accounts for C.S. Lewis and other authors)
- Celebration of church milestones
- Short homemade videos, perhaps just with a greeting
- Links to pro Christian videos (see ideas below)
- Links to great articles, songs, blogs or books
- Images of any event publicity, posters or flyers
- Links to mission organisations or missionary news
- Links to local events, celebrations or businesses
- Links to talks online, podcasts, the church website or other social media channels
- A homemade church photo booth or frame, which could be a great project for all ages

- Teasers for future events, talks or guests
- Prayers for national events or current affairs
- Questions about church, faith or theology
- Caption competitions for photos
- National church and denominational campaigns: use hashtags with relevant comment (for example, #TryAlpha, #ChristmasStarts or #EasterMeans)
- Links to local churches. Follow them, encourage them and share what they're doing; act like family
- Use generic popular hashtags like #TBT (Throw Back Thursday—an excuse to bring out the archive with photos, memories or songs)
- Repost something good from the past. It's allowed.

## Further reading on digital communications and church growth

- www.churchtrain.uk/resources
- www.dur.ac.uk/codec
- www.premierdigital.org.uk
- www.getyourchurchnoticed.com

# Online church comms communities

- Facebook for church communications: www.facebook.com/groups/churchcomm
- Facebook for church social media managers: www.facebook.com/groups/405311139621738
- Twitter chat: #chsocm (associated with www.churchsocmed.blogspot.co.uk); #ukchurchchat

# Scheduling tools

- Hootsuite
- Buffer
- Advice on how to create a social media posting schedule: bit.ly/2dw0yeO

# Free images for websites

- Freely: www.freelyphotos.com
- Unsplash: www.unsplash.com
- Wiki Commons: commons.wikimedia.org
- Flickr 'Creative Commons': flickr.com/creativecommons
- Google: in Google Images, click 'Search tools', then 'Usage rights', and choose from those 'labelled for reuse'
- www.photopin.com

- Stock Up: www.sitebuilderreport.com/stock-up
- churchm.ag/unsplash-alternatives
- More free images: bit.ly/1oPTEjO

## Advice on church copyright and data protection

London Diocese's parish communications toolkit has up-to-date sections on copyright and on data: bitly.com/ParishCommsToolkit.

On data protection, churches are subject to the rules set out by www.ico.gov.uk. A helpful briefing for churches is at bitly.com/StewardshipData.

For advice on music, lyrics and video, contact CCLI (01323 436100; ccli.com)

## Tools for creating social media graphics

- pablo.buffer.com
- spark.adobe.com
- canva.com
- bitly.com/ImageSizes2016 (for guidance on social media image sizes)

# More apps for adding words to images

- YouVersion (can add images behind Bible verses)
- Over
- Quick
- Typic
- PicLab
- Typorama

## Links for more about Christianity

- www.Christianity.org.uk
- www.lookingforGod.com
- www.justpray.uk
- www.alpha.org
- www.reJesus.co.uk
- www.knowmystory.co.uk

## Links for videos and testimonies

- www.yesheis.com
- Go Chatter channel on YouTube
- www.godtube.com
- www.greatcommission.co.uk

If you have more suggestions, add them to the toolkit at cpo.org.uk/toolkit.

# Notes

1   David Bourgeois, *Ministry in the Digital Age: Strategies and best practices for a post-website world* (IVP, 2013).

2   I'm grateful to David Giles for advance viewing of his paper 'Faith in Social Media', which seeks to fill the gap in research on the effectiveness of social media to convey faith messages.

3   Bryony Taylor remembers this quote from way back in 1999: 'Electronic evangelism is friendship evangelism via the internet.' Bryony Taylor, *Sharing Faith Using Social Media* (Grove Books, 2016), p. 8.

4   P. Phillips, B. Lewis and K. Bruce, 'Digital Communication, the Church and Mission', CODEC (St John's College Durham, 2013): www.churchgrowthrd.org.uk/UserFiles/File/ Resourcing_Mission_Bulletin/June_2013/Digital_ Communication_the_Church_and_Mission.pdf, p. 4 (my emphasis).

5   Tim Hutchings continues to do some fascinating research in this area. Also read Steve Aisthorpe's book *The Invisible Church* (St Andrew Press, 2016).

6   Brandon Cox, '4 Ways You Can Use Social Media for Good': www.smallgroups.com/articles/2015/4-ways-you-can-use-social-media-for-good. html?paging=off.

7   Find out more at www.ted.com.

8   Elizabeth Drescher, 'Digital ministry': www.
    faithandleadership.com/qa/elizabeth-drescher-
    digital-ministry-made-for-the-mainline.

9   Robin Ham, *Filtered Grace*: http://books.noisetrade.
    com/robinham/filtered-grace-reflections-on, p. 30.

10  Ian Jones (series ed.), *What Helps Disciples Grow?*,
    Faith and Learning Series 2 (St Peters Saltley, 2014).

11  The most recent stats on UK internet usage
    are found by searching for internet usage at
    www.ons.gov.uk. These were from: www.ons.
    gov.uk/peoplepopulationandcommunity/
    householdcharacteristics/
    homeinternetandsocialmediausage/bulletins/
    internetaccesshouseholdsandindividuals/
    2015-08-06; www.ons.gov.uk/
    businessindustryandtrade/itandinternetindustry/
    bulletins/internetusers/2016.

12  For up-to-date UK social media use, try www.
    wearesocial.com/uk and search for the most recent
    full digital report, which will have links to further
    data sources at the bottom.

13  www.dioceseofyork.org.uk/uploads/
    attachment/2688/social-media-guidelines.pdf, p. 1.

14  Quoted in Phillips, Lewis and Bruce, 'Digital
    Communication, the Church and Mission'.

15  Justin Wise, *The Social Church: A theology of digital
    communication* (Moody Press, 2014), p. 23.

16  Ed Brooks and Pete Nicholas, *Virtually Human* (IVP,
    2015), p. 29.

17  David Giles, 'Faith in Social Media' (www. faithinsocialmedia.org), p. 36, citing a ComRes report commissioned by Christian Vision in 2012.

18  Neil Pugmire, *100 Ways to Get Your Church Noticed* (Church House, 2014).

19  www.ons.gov.uk/businessindustryandtrade/ itandinternetindustry/bulletins/internetusers/2016.

20  www.ageuk.org.uk/work-and-learning/technology- and-internet/how-the-internet-changed-my-life.

21  www.thegiftofyears.org.uk.

22  BBC Radio 4, *Beyond Belief*, broadcast Monday 16 May 2016: www.bbc.co.uk/programmes/b07bbd4y.

23  Mumsnet: www.mumsnet.com/Talk/am_i_being_ unreasonable/a1499475-to-be-amazed-at-people- going-to-church.

24  Derek Ouellette, 'Why Some Churches Need to Stay Away from Social Media': www.derekouellette. ca/why-some-churches-need-to-stay-away-from- social-media.

25  Leon Watson, 'Humans Have Shorter Attention Span': www.telegraph.co.uk/science/2016/03/12/ humans-have-shorter-attention-span-than- goldfish-thanks-to-smart.

26  Read the full transcript or watch 'Connected, But Alone?' at www.ted.com/talks/sherry_turkle_ alone_together/transcript?language=en.

27  Tim Chester, *Will You Be My Facebook Friend?* (10Publishing, 2013).

28   Study of 2000 adults by Privilege home insurance, cited in *The Times*, 7 April 2016, p. 17. You can listen to a thoughtful reflection—and a call to use surveys like this carefully—from CODEC: www.premier.org.uk/News/UK/Christian-expert-Social-media-and-depression-not-clearly-linked.

29   More on this can be found, for example, in Eva Wiseman, 'The Ugly Truth about Body Dysmorphia': www.theguardian.com/lifeandstyle/2016/mar/06/the-ugly-truth-about-body-dysmorphia.

30   Bex Lewis, *Raising Children in a Digital Age* (Lion Hudson, 2014), ch. 12.

31   Wise, *The Social Church*, p. 132.

32   Pope Benedict XVI, *Social Networks: Portals of truth and faith; new spaces for evangelization* (Libreria Editrice Vaticana, 2013).

33   A worthwhile resource, even though written in 2009, is John Saddington, '12 Tips for Developing a Social Networking Policy and Usage Guidelines for Your Church': https://churchm.ag/12-tips-for-developing-a-social-networking-policy-and-usage-guidelines-for-your-church.

34   Derek Ouellette, '3 Social Media Mistakes Churches Make': www.churchtechtoday.com/2016/01/08/3-social-media-mistakes-churches-make.

35   The Smart Social Report Vol. 4: www.spredfast.com/social-media-white-paper/smart-social-report-volume-four.